✛

COPTIC ORTHODOX
PATRIARCHATE

See of St. Mark

WORDS

OF

SPIRITUAL BENEFIT

51-100
(Volume Two)

BY
H. H. POPE SHENOUDA III

Title: Words of Spiritual Benefit (Volume II)

Author: H. H. Pope Shenouda III.

Translation: Mrs. Bassilious, Australia

Revision: Dr. Angeile Botros Samaan, Professor of English Literature Cairo University

Press: Dar El Tebaa El Kawmia.

Edition: August 1989 - 2nd edition.

Legal deposit No.: 5608/1989.

Revised by: COEPA 1997

3

H.H. Pope Shenouda III, 117th Pope of
Alexandria and the See of St. Mark

CONTENTS

✣ ✣ ✣

IN THE NAME OF THE FATHER,
THE SON
AND THE HOLY SPIRIT.
ONE GOD AMEN.

INTRODUCTION

We meant to present 100 Words of Spiritual Benefit in two volumes, as indicated by the title of this book... But it seems that the talk between us is going to be long.

There is a third volume that has a special nature...

It will be published under the same title "Words of Spiritual Benefit" as Volume III of this series.

The main aim of publishing these books is for all of us to have one mind. This mind is to be, *"the mind of Christ"* (1 Cor. 2:16)

SHENOUDA III

51. IN THE WILDERNESS AND QUIETNESS

Amidst the hustle and bustle of life, with its many worries, how beautiful it is for one to devote even a little time, to sit with God, in an atmosphere of contemplation, prayer and open his heart to the Lord.

Here one resorts to calmness and quietness...

It is appropriate, when talking to God, to be alone with Him...

For this reason, God moved Abraham from his own country and people, to the mountain where he became alone with God... There, he had to build the Altar...

In the seclusion of the Holy Mountain, Moses spent forty days alone with God, till he took the Law and the Commandments and the instructions on how to build the tabernacle.

Also, in the seclusion of the mountain, the Lord Jesus met with His Disciples and sometimes He took them to an isolated place...

The prophet Elijah, was trained in the quietness of Mount Carmel.

John the Baptist, was brought up in the wilderness for thirty years.

The Prophets were also trained in quietness and calmness.

Moses, before he became a prophet and was chosen by God for leadership, spent forty years in quietness. He stayed far from Pharaoh's palace, with all its clamour and politics...

The Lord Jesus Himself, in spite of the unlimited tranquillity deep within Him and the eternal relationship with the Father, set the example for us by staying alone on the mountain for forty days in a state of quietness with the Father, before He started His public ministry.

The mountain had its place and position in the life of the Lord, as goes the beautiful saying of the Bible, *"And everyone went to his own house. But Jesus went to the Mount of Olives"* (John 8:1).

The garden of Gethsemane was a place of quietness as calmness for Christ, where He spent periods of deep contemplation.

Mary, the sister of Martha, was an example of the life of quietness, sitting calmly at the Lord's feet. As for her busy and worried sister, who was far from the life of quietness, the Lord rebuked her by saying, *"Martha, Martha, you are worried and troubled about many things. But one thing is needed..."* (Luke 10:40-41).

Then, will you search for the centre of quietness in your life?

Are you worried and troubled about many things... When will you calm down ... ? When?

52.   PREJUDICE

You might be a son of God, a servant of the Church, regular in doing spiritual deeds, but you are under the influence of prejudice, yielding to its effects ... !

Prejudice is to attack someone, without knowledge, without thinking and probably without reason ... !

At the same time, you support and defend someone, in the same way which is void of knowledge, thought or reason!

Prejudice has Paul and Apollos, which the Apostle criticised by rebuking the Corinthians, saying, *"For when one says, 'I am of Paul,' and another, 'I am of Apollos,' are you not carnal and behaving like mere men?"* (1 Cor. 3:4).

Prejudice does not agree with the spirit of love...

The person you criticise, attack and oppose, you definitely do not love... *"and love does not behave rudely, thinks no evil."* (1 Cor. 13:5).

Prejudice does not agree with truth and justice...

Mostly, attacks which fall in the sphere of prejudice, are not all true or just... At least they have a touch of exaggeration or incrimination, which is the outcome of spite in the heart...

Prejudice does not build but destroys...

It weakens strength and splits unity. It uses energy not in a natural course... but wastes it in quarrels, splits, criticism and contradiction.

Prejudice is against the unity of spirit and thought...

It is an embodiment of one's self... and does not agree with the Holy Church about whose children it was said *"Now the multitude of those who believed were of one heart and one soul."* (Acts 4:32).

Prejudice is against the command of the Apostles who said, *"...endeavouring to keep the unity of the Spirit, just as you were called in one hope of your calling, one Lord, one faith, one God, one baptism."* (Eph. 4:3-5).

Prejudice could adopt the spirit of competition or contradiction or contradiction to others and the spirit of boasting to oneself...

It could take an aspect of "worshipping of heroes" or belonging to the public.

All that remains in your sight is our group, our society, our branch, our church (on the district level), our country, our village...

✥

53. DIVISION

One of the saints once said, "If ten thousand angels assembled together, they would have one opinion, but when few humans gather together, they disagree!..

Division could be an evidence of the existence of the self...

The self that works on its own, far from the Spirit of God:

✛   which aims at enforcing its own opinion, no matter what the outcome would be...

✛ which does not care about the dangerous results that are caused by division!

What are these consequences?... A writer once said, "Two eagles had a fight over a prey, it was taken by the fox".

For this, the Lord Jesus said, *"Every city or house divided against itself will not stand."* (Matt. 12:25). Splitters always forget this saying.

Very often, a group would take an act of division and leave behind a ruined atmosphere, then goes its own way as if it has done nothing! But God seeks the blood of what its actions destroyed...

Division among brothers is a sign of lack of love...

The division of the young against the old means rebellion, lack of obedience and lack of respect to superiors... These are all sins.

Division also proves pride in oneself or self importance. Most likely, the confession Father is left out of all this; he is not consulted...

In St. Paul's Epistle to the Corinthians, he rebuked them for their division and described them as being carnal (1 Cor. 3), as the splitters are far from the unity of the Spirit.

Members of the one body collaborate together for the good of that body.

If they all felt this unity, they would work jointly for the good that everyone is aiming at.

Unity needs respecting others' opinion, or at least training oneself to do so, without revolt, anger, defamation of others or destruction...

A piece of advice to anyone who leads a way of division:
✤　　**Try to gain others instead of splitting from them.**
✤　　**Be objective and stay away from personal affairs.**
✤　　**Train yourself to cooperate with the spirit of a group.**

✤ ✤ ✤

54.   HE WHO LIKES TO BENEFIT

The one who likes to benefit always searches for profitability. Too much talk does not profit him, but one word could change his whole life... He even benefits from silence, as St. Paphnoti said about one of his guests, "If he does not profit from my silence, then he would not profit from my talk either."

St. Anthony heard one phrase and it was the cause of his monasticism and the foundation of this angelic rite. Another phrase made him go to the inner wilderness and the life of solitude.

God does not stipulate to teach you by many words, one phrase will suffice. The Ten Commandments are all short sentences, but carry all the teachings.

The Lord's prayer has short phrases that carry the depth of supplications.

The one who likes to benefit seeks the profitability at any price.

The spirit-borne used to endure the hardships of long travels to hear one word from one of the Fathers. The Fathers themselves used to benefit from any one or even from their children.

The one who asks for good always finds it...

Even in a passing word, from anyone, in a casual incident that accidentally happened to him or others. He profits from his own and other people's mistakes.

One of the Saints once said, "I don't remember the devil tempting me to the same sin twice," because he benefited from his fall and was careful in the second...

The Lord Jesus asked us to learn from the lilies of the fields and the birds of the sky and learn a lesson in faith and in God's care.

Sources of profit are available: not only in the words of a preacher, or in spiritual books, but they are also everywhere and at anytime. The main point is: do you want to profit or not.

God's voice reaches everyone, in different ways. But, *"He who has ears to hear, let him hear."* (Matt. 11:15).

55. SERIOUS WORK

The Bible says, *"Cursed is he who does the work of the Lord deceitfully."* (Jer. 48:10)...

The one who works for the Lord must, *"Be faithful until death."* (Rev. 2:10). Faithfulness is a principal condition for service...

With this seriousness, the Apostles witnessed for the name of Christ and they were, *"Preaching the Kingdom of God... with all confidence, no one forbidding them."* (Acts 28:31) *"And with great power, the Apostles gave witness... and great grace was upon them all."* (Acts 4:33).

As a result of this serious, honest and faithful work, the kingdom of God spread. Listen to what God said to the angle of the Church of Ephesus.

"I know your works, your labour, your patience... and you have persevered and have patience and have laboured for my name's sake and have not become weary." (Rev. 2:2-3).

Serious work is built on faith...

The more your faith in the weight and importance of your work is true and complete, the more the seriousness of your work will be. Lenience in work is an evidence of lack of faith and its importance...

Serious work indicates a sense of responsibility:

Just as what Joseph, the faithful, did, stockpiling wheat, fully aware that the life of many depends on his honesty.

So it is with the spiritual service: the life of many depends on the honesty of the servant. If he neglects his service they are lost.

Serious work is controlled from one's inner self...

It is controlled by one's own conscience and the voice of God inside him.

This control is due to his live feelings and holy zeal...

He works seriously because "Time is short" and every minute counts, with any delay or negligence having its danger...

Serious work is always successful...

It is a perfect work because seriousness brings work to perfection...

Perfect work is a successful work. It was said about the righteous men, *"And whatever he does shall prosper."* (Ps. 1:3).

Serious work does not slow down till completed...

It does not believe in fatigue and does not seek rest ...

Its performer does not rest until the work is finished and he tastes its fruits... Like Lazarus of Damascus who would not rest till he took Rachel as wife for his master's son. And when they asked him to rest, he answered *"Do not hinder me."* (Gen. 24:56).

56.   I ALONE

At one time, Elijah thought that he was the only one worshipping God, as he said, "... And I alone am left..." But God told him that seven thousand men have not bowed the knee to Baal.

How dangerous is the feeling that we are the only ones worshipping God, or the only ones with principles!!

We tend to forget that there are seven thousand knees (which is the multiple of an even number) who worship God and we are not aware...

There are those who judge the whole generation and judge all people as being lost and corrupted!! They forget that there are those who are chosen by God, whom they might not know, but God knows them.

The scribes and pharisees used to think that they were the only ones who knew the law and stuck strictly to the statute. Therefore, they were struck by pride and arrogance of the heart and raised themselves above others. They began to judge others and describe them as being sinners. They even accused the Lord Jesus of breaking the Sabbath and violating the Law. They also criticised Him for humbly sitting with tax collectors and sinners...

When St. Anthony was attacked by self-righteousness and thought that he was the only monk, God sent him to where St. Paul was, to show him the one who was better than him...

When St. Macarius the Great was attacked in the same way, God sent him to two married women in Alexandria who according to God's words were on the same spiritual level as him. He was not the only one and these two were of the seven thousand hidden knees...

How painful is this sin, when one thinks that he is the only honest servant, the only one who has talents, principles and ideals, while others have none. He is the only right person for leadership and nobody else!

The one who has love rejoices at having many like him or even better than him... As Moses said, *"Oh, that all the land's people were prophets..."* (Num. 11:29). As for the self-conceited, this matter troubles him, or at least does not cheer him ... ! He thinks it is a challenge to him. He does not even care about God, but about himself...

57.   DREAMS

1. Some dreams are from God:

Such as what happened with Joseph, the Carpenter and the
Magi. Joseph, in a dream, was told to take the child and his
mother and go to Egypt. The Magi were asked, in a dream, to
return by a different route.

Further the dreams that were seen or interpreted by Joseph, the
righteous, or Daniel the Prophet.   They were all dreams
predicting future incidents.

2.   There are dreams from Satan:

They deceive man and lead him astray, make him take a sinful
way or disturb him by certain dreams. In "The Sayings of the
Desert Fathers", there is a long chapter about such dreams.

3.   Some dreams are the outcome of the subconscious:

Whatever you see, hear or read, is gathered by the senses from
different sources and what the thought collects... all remains
stored in the subconscious... It comes out, even after years, in
the form of thoughts, doubts or dreams...

This is a very natural reaction...

This stock in the subconscious could come out in different forms... Names, times, places or some details might differ, but it presents something that is deeply rooted inside you, like a recorded tape...

4.   Dreams could be a reflection of a physical position:

When an exhausted person goes to sleep and the alarm clock rings, since he does not want to wake up, he dreams of sitting next to a ringing telephone...

A wise person does not let dreams lead him.

He would not believe each dream and consider it from God, because if the devils knew that he would believe in dreams, they will deceive him by appearing in false dreams.

Evil dreams happen for many reasons...

Some reasons are physical or psychological, others are attacks from devils. It is better if one does not think of these dreams after waking up, lest his thoughts result in its confirmation and cause others...

58.   PERSONAL THOUGHTS

Many people are fond of publishing their personal thoughts and presenting them to others as spiritual principles or beliefs essential to be followed...

The more these thoughts are new and unknown, the more they become pleased as they are presenting something new which makes them knowledgeable in the eyes of others!

The more this new knowledge is different from what people know and believe in, the more these thinkers are happy. To them it is like abolishing a general concept which is wrong and setting a new, correct one in its place.

This system might work in any type of knowledge, but never in beliefs; by destroying an ancient belief to build a new one on its ruins ...!

The older a belief is, the firmer it is...

Whatever is new in a belief could be a heresy if it destroys an old one that has been passed to us by our forefathers.

Therefore, those who favour their own thoughts, try their best to find old manuscripts to back them... And if they fail they fabricate it...

Such people do not read the "Sayings of the Fathers", to understand their thoughts... but they only read, hunting for a saying or a phrase to support them...

They cut off this text, separating it from what is before or after it, isolating it from the occasion in which it was said and the general line of thought of the father from whom it was taken... They use this quotation as a means of confirming their thoughts, even though the writings of this saint could be contradictory to the sayings they related to him.

They do not search for the truth but for what supports their thoughts, no matter how this evidence could be fabricated and incorrect.

As for you blessed son, when it comes to matters relating to doctrine and faith, do not publish a personal thought, but what the church believes in...

Do not spread any new idea that comes to your thinking but refer it to those responsible in the church to have their say before it is spread to the people.

Teaching in church is not a field for displaying personal thoughts, but it is a field for a unison teaching which takes its origin from the Apostolic tradition, one faith for all...

✠ ✠ ✠

59. QUIETNESS

St. Peter, the Apostle, talked about, *".. a gentle and quiet spirit, which is very precious in the sight of God."* (1 Pet. 3:4).

St. Paul also advised us about this quietness by saying, *"...that you also aspire to lead a quiet life.."* (1 Thess. 4:11).

There are many types of quietness, one of which is quietness of nerves.

Such nerves do not turn to anger or get agitated quickly. They do not become enraged but handle problems quietly and by a gentle answer, eliminate anger, as the wise man said.

The Bible says, *"But the wicked are like the troubled sea, when it cannot rest, whose waters cast up mire and dirt. There is no peace, says my God, for the wicked."* (Is. 57:20-21).

Another type of quietness is that of the heart..

One might control his outer reactions, while his heart is in fury inside. A truly quiet person would be quiet on the outside as well as on the inside.

Quietness of the heart includes being quiet when facing anger, fear, doubt, jealousy as well as other emotions, desires and inner wars that cause violent struggles inside a person.

This quietness is part of the inner peace…

And from quietness of the heart, springs quietness of the thought …

A quiet, balanced thought that work without excitement or disturbance, enables one to think far from any clamour or agitation.

This quietness of thinking enables one to reach wisdom and as said in the Bible, *"Words of the wise, spoken quietly, should be heard rather than the shout of a ruler of fools."* (Eccl. 9:17).

Quietness of the senses helps to achieve quietness of the thought.

Therefore, our Fathers sought a life of quietness, knowing that by a quiet body, one obtains a quiet spirit.

One of the most beautiful sayings of the Bible about the usefulness of quietness is, *"For thus says the Lord God. In returning and rest you shall be saved; In quietness and confidence shall be your strength."* (Is. 30:15).

Let us be eager to live a life of quietness and seek it from God.

✠ ✠ ✠

60. THE GOOD MEANS

It is not enough that the work we do is good in itself or in its objectives, but the means we use must be kind and good.

For example, violence and extreme strictness and cruelty are not all good ways of upbringing or achieving discipline and obedience.

Mostly these are displeasing means that do not suit every person. One might arrive at his aim without violence or cruelty... by adopting good means...

Swearing, also, is not a spiritual way of answering those who disagree with you in faith or in opinion.

By doing this you lose the one whom you agree with and if you were a writer or an author you will also lose your readers. The correct way is to be objective in the discussion of matters concerning faith and beliefs, without swearing or insults, because, *"... nor revilers nor extortioners will inherit the kingdom of God."* (1 Cor. 6:10).

Destruction, bitter criticism or trying to ruin others, are not good means of expressing holy zcal.

Zeal could be shown in a positive and constructive way that handles matters deliberately and objectively. It could also be shown by quiet study and submission of acceptable solutions that are done in love. As it says in the Bible, *"Let all that you do be done in love."* (1 Cor. 16:14).

Division is not a good way for ecclesiastical work or even for social and national work.

Division weakens the ranks and proves lack of cooperation and inability to deal with the other point of view. It could also be an evidence of failure in convincing and gaining the other side.

The Bible says, *"And he who wins souls is wise."* (Prov. 11:30).

The wise chooses right means for his good deeds.

Wrong means do not go with good work.

And the good work, if achieved through improper means, becomes a combination of light and darkness or mixture of virtue and sin and would not prove to be spiritual.

Let our means be good, quiet and spiritual, at least, let them not be harmful or a stumbling block.

61   THE BASIC VIRTUES

Some virtues are partial and one struggles hard to attain them, but there are basic virtues which include various merits within them; ...

Above all virtues is: Love.

The Lord Jesus Christ said that all the Law and prophets are concerned with this virtue.

St. Paul explained the various sorts of the virtue of love and said, *"Love suffers long and is kind, love does not envy, love does not parade itself, is not puffed up, does not behave rudely, does not seek its own, is not provoked, thinks no evil, does not rejoice in iniquity but rejoices in the truth, bears all things, believes all things, hopes all things, endures all things.   Love never fails."* (1 Cor. 13:4-8).

Therefore, whoever has love, has all these virtues.

All that St. Paul mentioned was our love to our neighbours...

As for our love to God, no doubt, it includes various matters:

It includes Prayer with all its levels, contemplation, deliberation, reading the Bible, loving the church and its sacraments, spiritual gatherings, fasting, prostrating... it also includes following all commandments as God says, *"He who has my commandments and keeps them, it is he who loves me."* (John 14:21).

Another leading virtue is the life of submission...

Submission means the complete surrender of one's self to the Holy Spirit that works in his heart, to run his life...

This person will show the fruits of the Holy Spirit that St. Paul explained in Galatians 5:22, by saying, "But the fruit of the Spirit is love, joy, peace, long-suffering, kindness, goodness, faithfulness, gentleness and self control."

One of the mother virtues is also humility...

A humble person acquires gentleness quietness, stays away from anger and judging others and keeps himself from cruelty...

Humility also includes contrition of heart, self reproach, the virtue of tears, love, blessing everyone, seeking the blessings of everyone, listening more than talking, never boasting or elevating oneself or self praising, contentment with everything, satisfaction, thankfulness and simplicity.

✛ ✛ ✛

62.   THE LOVE OF PROFIT

The one who loves to profit would benefit from everything, from everyone and from any incident.

He finds an advantage in everything he experiences.

He profits from the good and also from the bad...

From the righteous person, he takes a good example, love and good treatment. From the evil person he attains the virtues of patience, endurance and forgiveness... Also, you can learn any virtue when you know the harms and disadvantages of the corresponding vice.

A wise man said, "I learned silence from a pratter."

Therefore, realising the disadvantages of pratting enabled me to know the advantages of silence and to avoid such evils...

We can learn from our mistakes as well as from the faults of others...

The wise person knows how to profit from mistakes so he will not fall into them once more and gains experience in life. A person with many experiences is a source of benefit.

The one who wants to profit can also profit from nature, not only from those he meets.

The wise man said, "Go to the ant you sluggard, consider her ways and be wise." It is really beautiful to see the ant as a source of benefit for us.

As we benefit from nature we can also benefit from incidents... either what happens to us or to others. They are all useful lessons in life, for those who are keen to learn...

The story of the rich fool was a lesson for many... All the stories and events recorded in the Bible are also lessons, just like historical incidents. As the poet says, "whoever keeps history in his heart, adds ages to his age."

Spiritual fathers are not the only source of benefit.

As far as the heart is searching for benefit, God will surely send it in various ways and means...

63.   THE CROSS

The Cross is a symbol of suffering and three crosses symbolise three cases:

The Cross of Christ is a symbol of suffering for righteousness' sake, while the other two crosses refer to suffering as a penalty for sin. These are divided into two kinds: one suffers because of his sins then repents and returns while the other suffers because of his sins but complains and grumbles, then dies in his sins...

The Cross which is for righteousness' sake is also of a different kind:

The cross of love and sacrifice is like the Cross of Christ who endured suffering to save us, *"Greater love has no one than this, to lay down his life for his friends."* (John 15:13).

There is another cross in offering.   And the greatest offering is that given from the needs where you prefer others to yourself. You become in need to let others take, like the widow who gave all that she had, her whole livelihood.

Another Cross is that of endurance: turning the other cheek and walking the second mile. It is not only bearing people's abuses, but being good to those who spitefully use you and also loving them!...

Who can do that?... It is a cross...

There is another cross in the Spiritual Struggle: in the victory of the spirit over the body, in enduring the hardships and wars of the world, the body and the devil... It is also in crucifying the body and its desires,... having victory over oneself.... entering through the narrow gate...

It is a Cross to suffer for righteousness' sake. This is only for beginners... As for the perfect, the cross turns into joy and pleasure...

We feel the narrowness of the gate at the beginning of the way. But later on, we find pleasure in carrying out the commandment and love it. By then the way would not be distressful and what at first was a cross becomes a pleasure...

Martyrdom used to be a Cross, then it turned to be a joy. Saints began to desire martyrdom and long for death and rejoice in it...

Labouring and suffering for God's sake became a pleasure and an enjoyment.

Therefore, the Bible considers suffering a gift from God...

"For to you it has been granted on behalf of Christ, not only to believe in him, but also to suffer for his sake." (Phil. 1:29).

When will the cross be a joy in our life?

✠ ✠ ✠

64. FAITH

Faith is not just a set of rigid beliefs that we learn by heart from theology and the teachings of the church. Rather faith is a deep inner conviction and complete confidence in God, His attributes and His work.

Our faith in God, His existence, care and protection gives us inner peace and comfort in the heart and in the mind. It gives us confidence that as far as God exists. He cares about us more than we do about ourselves. Therefore we have to live in this peace and continue in it.

The faithful never become disturbed because anxiety contradicts faith... faith in God's love, care and protection...

If one believed in God's existence everywhere, one would have an inner feeling of the holiness of any place, since God is always there. As he feels secure in the presence of God, he also feels the necessity to be precise in all his actions, knowing that God sees, hears and observes all his deeds...

In every sin, one says with the righteous Joseph, *"How then can I do this great wickedness and sin against God?"* (Gen. 39:9).

One's faith that God reads one's thoughts and knows the secrets of his heart, his intentions and feelings; such faith grants him modesty in his thoughts and feelings, making him bashful of God who examines all these emotions...

One's faith in the world to come and the day of judgement when he gives an account of all his deeds, thoughts, feelings and sayings, makes him sure of this perishable world. One then sees the need to be prepared for that fearful day working for eternal life after death...

One keeps this thought in his heart saying with David, *"Lord make me to know my end and what is the measure of my days, that I may know how frail I am."* (Ps. 39:4).

Faith is not just to be mentally convinced but is an action inside the heart, to lead one through his whole life...

It is not a specific moment where Man accepts God. It is a life-time job, where one lives in confidence that, *"Faith is the substance of things hoped for, the evidence of things not seen."* (Heb. 11:1).

Therefore, the word faith in most cases means the whole Christian life with all its beliefs and deeds...

65.   PRAYER

Prayer, in its simple meaning, is a talk with God... In its deeper meaning, it is a relationship with God...

It is a relationship of love and emotions before being words. A talk without love is meaningless.

Therefore, God says in reproach, *"In as much as these people draw near to me with their mouths and honour me with their lips, but have removed their hearts far from me."* (Is. 29:13).

For this reason, the prayer of the evil is not accepted before God. It is hated by God because it is not the outcome of love, except if it is a contrite evil person who is asking for forgiveness like the tax-collector.

God said about those who pray without being pure in heart, *"When you spread out your hands, I will hide my eyes from you, even though you make many prayers, I will not hear. Your hands are full of blood. Wash yourselves clean; put away the evil of your doings from before my eyes. Cease to do evil."* (Is. 1:15-16).

Prayer is a bridge connecting Earth to Heaven. It has been compared to Jacob's ladder that connected Heaven to

Earth. Prayer is a key to Heaven, it is the language and job of Angels and it is the life of the spirituals.

Prayer is one's longing to be with God. It is the longing of the limited to the unlimited, the creature to the Creator, the soul to its source and its satisfaction...

In prayer, one is elevated above materialism to meet with God.

As a measurement for the success of prayer, one feels unable to finish and stop praying. The opposite happens with the one who is happy to conclude his prayer and say amen.

The one who is successful in his prayers would be unable to leave it. Instead, he sings his favourite song with the Angels, *"I held him and would not let him go."* (Song 3:4).

Whoever succeeds in praying would never prefer any other work whatsoever to it. For prayer's sake, saints escaped the world and all worldly things searching for quietness and silence, which they loved with all their hearts, to be alone with God.

Prayer is a taste of God's Kingdom, which starts here and finishes there.

If one becomes attached to it, prayer becomes a life to him and his life becomes a prayer...

There is a saint whose whole life is written in one phrase, so we say, "His life was a prayer." It is a continuous, uninterrupted prayer that has not stopped for a second to give the singer time to say "selah". Even in his sleep one's talk with God does not stop, in the conscious and the unconscious. Does it explain the verse, *"When I remember you on my bed?"* (Ps. 63:6).

66. LIFE OF SACRIFICE

All that God asks from you is your heart, *"My son, give me your heart."* (Prov. 23:26)... When He asks for your heart, He asks for your love. The evidence of love is sacrifice.

Therefore a spiritual life is a life of sacrifice, offering everything even life itself. *"It is more blessed to give than to receive."* (Acts 20:35).

You have to give up something for the sake of God, to move your love for Him. Your love is as great as what you give up for God's sake.

Look at Abraham, the father of fathers, how did he start his relationship with God ...? It started with God saying to him, *"Get out of your country, from your kindred and from your father's house, to a land I will show you."* (Gen. 12:1).

For God's sake, Abraham left his family and his country. Was God satisfied with that? No! Even in the strange land, God said to him, *"Take now your son, your only son Isaac, whom you love and offer him as a burnt offering."* (Gen. 22:2). Abraham obeyed and went to offer his son...

Moses also sacrificed his princely position, the royal palace and all the riches and authority *"...esteeming the reproach of Christ greater riches than the treasures in Egypt."* (Heb. 11:26).

The Apostles said to the Lord Jesus "We have left all and followed you" and St. Paul the Apostle said, *"... for when I have suffered the loss of all things and count them as rubbish, that I may gain Christ."* (Phil. 13:8).

Sacrifice reaches its peak when you offer everything: like the widow who paid the coins and the widow who gave the prophet Elijah all the food she had. *"Go sell whatever you have and give to the poor and come take the cross and follow me."* (Mark 10:21).

God himself gave us this love as an example of sacrifice, *"For God so loved the world that he gave his only son."* (John 3:16) *"Greater love has no one than this, to lay down his life for his friends."* (John 15:13).

The martyrs gave themselves up to death and did not love their life because of their love for the Lord Jesus Christ.

What about you dear reader?... What have you sacrificed for the sake of Christ who gave Himself up and became man and died on the cross?

We do not ask you to sacrifice your life like the martyrs, as it was a special time. **The most important thing to give up for His sake is your favourite sins.**

✠ ✠ ✠

67. COMPLETENESS IN VIRTUE

Being literal in virtue spoils it. Wisdom gives virtue a stronger and practical meaning...

The virtue of tolerance and patience is an example, *"In your patience possess your souls."* (Luke 21:19) And by giving yourself time, you will be able to solve many problems. Being hasty and impatient could be devised by the devil, beside making one disturbed and restless.

Nevertheless, there are matters that need prompt action...

Without being quick, a matter would lead to tragedy or loss...

For example, seeking and saving sinners, removing a person from a sinful place, solving a family problem before it gets more complicated and reaches court, reprimanding a person guilty of sin, before he becomes a danger to others and get more in delinquency... all such matters need urgent action.

Repentance also does not work with patience and waiting...

The virtue of patience and tolerance, on its own, would not be beneficial without wisdom, as being literal does not work...

Many are the faults that we fall in if we separate wisdom from the virtue of gentleness and quietness, without considering the surrounding circumstances...

There are certain situations of holy zeal for which patience and gentleness would not work but they require some holy anger. Such anger must be mingled with purity of the heart to comply with the Bible's saying, *"Be angry and do not sin."* (Ps. 4:4).

For this reason there must he completeness in virtues and none of them should go alone.

Zeal completes wisdom and wisdom completes patience.

As we talk about God's attributes by saying: God is just in His mercy and merciful in His justice. God's justice is full of mercy and His mercy is full of justice.

In God, perfection is found and in Man, there is completeness...

68   FEASTS OF THE SAINTS

Feasts of the Saints are occasions for gatherings of many of the faithful who seek the intercession of these Saints in the fullness of faith:

They have faith in the Saints' intimacy with God, and God's acceptance of their prayers and intercessions. It is also faith in the eternity of the spirit and its work after death and the continuous relationship between the church on earth and the spirits of the Saints who have departed.

Many miracles happen during the feasts, as result of people's faith and God granted them their hearts' desire. It would have been very proper to record all the miracles that happened during the feasts of the Saints, as evidence to strengthen everybody's faith and show them that the age of miracles is not over yet and it is not restricted to the early ages...

The church has benefited from these large gatherings during the feasts of the Saints by having a spiritual revival and useful programmes to deepen faith and lead people spiritually.

Therefore, the church stopped all kinds of amusement and play and performed daily Masses. An internal broadcasting unit has been organised for the feast of each Saint, to broadcast hymns, sermons and spiritual teachings for different walks of life... These programmes vary to cover subjects which concern families, children, youth, women and workers...

There has also been expansion to benefit from audio visual aids by showing interesting religious films and slides. This resulted in building necessary halls for such shows...

The church also prints and distributes useful pamphlets and displays souvenirs such as crosses, icons and pictures.

People started spending consecrated spiritual periods during these feasts from which they gain great spiritual benefits.

Feasts of the Saints are also occasions for the faithful to become united. It is one of the characteristics of the practical orthodox life...

It is an evidence that the church is one, in Heaven and on Earth, in this life and the life to come...

Feasts of the Saints are a great blessing, especially after the attention given to them by the Bishops, particularly the historical churches that our people visit, to feel their holiness and spiritual effect.

69   WORKING WITH GOD

The Lord Jesus said, *"My Father has been working until now and I have been working."* (John 5:17). Let us concentrate on the last phrase...

St. Paul said about himself and his companion Apollos, *"For we are God's fellow workers."* (1 Cor. 3:9).

God can do everything on his own, but he wants you to work with Him, not only to work, but to toil and strive, *"And each one will receive his own reward according to his own labour."* (1 Cor. 3:8).

The fact that God works does not mean than Man becomes slack...

God, in Revelation, blessed the Angel of the church in Ephesus for labouring and toiling, saying, *"I know your works, your labour, your patience and that you cannot bear those who are evil and you have persevered and have patience and have laboured for my name's sake and have not become weary."* (Rev. 2:2-3).

Work for the spiritual person, is an association with God and the Holy Spirit. It is a partnership with the Divine Nature in work... It is the readiness of one's will, not only to associate with God but to become actually a partner...

Therefore we say to God in the Liturgy of the travellers, "Share in the work of your servants."

Depending on God does not mean idleness or carelessness but it is an association with God; relying on God's strength.

Through work, God tests the extent of our love and obedience to Him. And as St. John the Apostle said, *"Let us not love in word or in tongue, but in deed and in truth."* (1 John 3:18).

In spite of David's faith that, "the war is for God" and his confidence that God is going to work with him, he took his sling and stones and progressed to the front to face Goliath...

Therefore, you must work and ask God to be with you in what you are doing. But beware of idleness, as God does not like the sluggard...

You have to plant and water then God will make the plant grow...

Truly, you could humbly say, *"So then neither he who plants is anything, nor he who waters, but God gave the increase."* (1 Cor. 3:7).

✢ ✢ ✢

70. EXAMINE YOUR WAY

There is a kind of person who rushes on his way and would not change it, no matter what happens!

He stubbornly insists on his way, even after it is proved wrong and would not lead to any satisfactory result.

He thinks that dignity is to be firm, even in what is wrong, as Herod did when he killed John the Baptist!

He considers changing one's way a kind of hesitancy that does not go in line with strength and firmness!

It is a type of stubbornness that some people adopt and never change despite the fact that it becomes obvious that it is harmful for them and their followers.

Some might continue in such a way for years... It might be a conflict or a lawsuit that drags for years...
It could be a lost case, but he would not give up... Or, it could be a matter of a relationship that some would keep, even though it would not end well...

As for you, examine your way from time to time...

There is nothing wrong in evaluating the situation and

its surroundings and the anticipated consequences. Then one would be able to see the necessary action, suitable for the time being, not the past...

Examining one's way is wise...

The important thing is not to stick to one, but to make sure that this is the right way.

The way is merely the means to reach an aim.

You have then to be more concerned about the aim and objective, choosing the suitable means to achieve it.

Many wasted their life because of obstinacy and stubbornness...

Others destroyed many with them, following the same course...

Both groups probably lived without guidance...

They depended on their own thoughts, or more correctly on their emotions. So they wasted life unwisely and in vain...

71.   BENEFITING FROM MISTAKES

Everyone is liable to err but a wise person benefits from his mistakes. He gains spiritual experience, knowledge and care not to sin in the future. In this respect, one of the fathers said, "I do not remember the devil agitating me with the same sin twice."...

A spiritual person attains humility through his faults...

He realises and becomes aware of his weakness and how he is liable to make mistakes like others. He would not be proud or arrogant or think himself special. As St. Paul the Apostle said, *"Therefore let him who thinks he stands take heed lest he fall."* (1 Cor. 10:12).

When the ignorant person falls, he could weaken and continue in his fault becoming used to falling. He might despair, gets depressed and collapses.

As for the wise man, he understands the devils' tricks and combats through his sin. He learns how the devil gets to the human soul and becomes more precautions and precise. It might even help him to guide others, as he becomes more aware of the way...

A spiritual person benefits from his mistakes through sympathy with others, as the Apostle says, *"Remember the* *prisoners as if chained with them and those who are mistreated, since you yourselves are in the body also."* (Heb. 13:3).

Therefore, when the spiritual person fails, he becomes more sympathetic towards others without judging or rebuking, as he himself knows the power of devils and the weakness of human nature.

The spiritual person benefits from his mistakes by the practice of praying for himself and others. He is completely certain that man's victory does not depend on his strength and cleverness, but on God's help, as He leads us to victory. Therefore, one gets more attached to prayer, saying to God, *"Hold me up and I shall be safe."* (Ps. 119:117) and *"Our God will fight for us."* (Neh. 4:20).

The one who searches for benefit, profits from his mistakes as well as others' mistakes...

Therefore, God permitted in His Holy Bible to mention others' mistakes, even those of prophets and righteous people, so we may benefit from their mistakes...

Our God who said, *"And out of the strong came something sweet"* (Judg. 14:14) is also able to give us a useful lesson from each sin, for the salvation of ourselves...

Thus we benefit from all those we meet in life, from the righteous we take an example and from our sins and those of others, we gain experience and cautiousness...

✠ ✠ ✠

72.   GROWTH

One of the characteristics of the spiritual life is continual growth...

Man starts his relationship with God through repentance then he grows from the fear of God to His love. The growth in love continues till it reaches holiness, as it is said in the Bible..."you also be holy in all your conduct, because it is written, *'Be holy for I am holy'".* (1 Pet. 1:15-16).

Would one stop after reaching holiness?

No he has to strive for perfection.

The Bible says, *"Therefore you shall be perfect, just as your Father in heaven is perfect."* (Matt. 5:48).

The one who endeavours on the road to perfection never reaches its end, no matter how far he gets, perfection has no limits...

There are levels of perfection, each level is higher than the other...

Look at St. Paul, who was a saint. He was caught up to the third heaven and he made wonders and miracles.

In spite of all that, he says, *"Not that I have already attained, or am already perfected; but I press on... I do not count myself to have apprehended; but one thing I do, forgetting those things which are behind and reaching forward to those things which are ahead."* (Phil. 3:12-13).

The Apostle concludes his saying about this growth, "Therefore, let us, as many as are mature, have this mind."

We can see that even the righteous must always strive, "to reach forward."

God has compared the faithful to a grain of wheat that becomes a seedling and grows. He said, *"... and the seed should sprout and grow, he himself does not know how. For the earth yields crops by itself; first the blade, then the head and after that the full grain in the head."* (Mark 4:27-28).

Are you like the wheat that grows continually, starting as a seedling becoming an ear of corn then full grains of wheat ?...

Try to grow as growth gives continual warmth. To stop growing means no warmth in the heart which leads to one's lukewarmness.

If you feel you are unable to grow, try at least to stop where you are. Beware of going backwards.

✣ ✣ ✣

73.   THE LATE THOUGHT

Sometimes, one takes an action instead of thinking of its results first; he works without any consideration of the consequences. Then after it is done, he starts thinking of the outcome when it is too late.

This kind of late thinking is wrong...

Another person makes vows without thinking if it is within his ability to fulfil them or not... And after making the vow, he starts thinking, tries to change it or declares his inability...

It is late thinking that happens after its proper time.

A wife could lose her husband, through certain ways of treatment, or taking the wrong advice from a relative, making her lose his love.   Then she refuses any interference for reconciliation.   After her husband reaches the point that his life with her is unbearable, she begins to think that losing him is not in her favour...

But this is a late consideration which comes too late.

A father fails in raising his son properly, thinking that pampering is a sign of love.   So the child grows up used to disobedience, recklessness and carelessness.   These faults become deeply rooted in his personality, causing bitterness in the heart of his father, mother, sisters and all those connected to him. By that time, the father starts thinking of changing his method of upbringing and turns to strictness after it becomes too late...

The father fails because his thinking was late.

It is not enough for one to have good thoughts. This thinking ought to he alert, right from the beginning, not after missing the chance...

The foolish virgins returned to God with their lamps, but after the door was shut... They did not enter.

The virgin of the song arose to open the door for her beloved, but after he had turned away and was gone. Therefore she says, *"My heart went out to him when he spoke. I sought him, but I could not find him; I called him, but he gave me no answer."* (Song 5:6).

Many started thinking late, so they did not benefit and lived in continual regret and sorrow... It is like what happened to Esau who cried with an exceedingly great and bitter cry of repentance but it was not given to him. Esau came after Jacob took away his birthright and his blessing. The matter was all over.

How beautiful is the psalm that says, *"Early will I seek you"* (Ps. 63:1) and how it is that, *"... those who seek me diligently will find me."* (Prov. 8:17). They think early.

✢ ✢ ✢

74. AT THE END OF THE YEAR

We do not want the New Year to take you by surprise without being prepared for its beginning. We are drawing your attention to this matter so that you can make yourself ready...

✢ **Sit first with yourself, to know its sincerity...** it is not only to know its faults, but mostly to know its basic areas of weakness... its causes and its substances...

According to the outcome of this sitting with yourself, you become prepared for confession especially the deep confession that deals with everything in your life, more than the parts... the roots more than the branches...

✢ At the end of the year, study what should be done to make it a holy year in everything, then say the beautiful phrase by which we start the morning prayer in the Agbia, "Let us enjoy a fresh start..."

✢ **Let us observe the characteristics of the Christian life, the basics, not the deviations in the daily life.**

Where is the centre of God's Love in your life?

Where is the centre of Faith? Gentleness? Humility? Hope?

How deep is your relationship with God?

Enter into the depth and do not be shallow in your spirituality or superficially estimate yourself.

✥   Look at yourself as a whole and the extent of its development...

Which way does the spiritual side in your life go?

Are you taking a clear, firm way, in which you are progressing and growing day after day?

Or is there a change, an alteration and a deviation from the holy path; new things that came into you, when they shouldn't!

✥   A principal piece of advice I give you to keep in your mind while sitting with yourself and with God:

Be honest to the fullest...

Beware of justifying yourself, finding excuses and putting the blame on others or on circumstances!

On the day of judgement, God is not going to ask you about the circumstances or about others. He is going to ask you about yourself.

Enter then inside yourself and yourself only, nothing else.

✥ ✥ ✥

75. THE FAITHFUL OVER A LITTLE

Be faithful over a little, God will set you over much...

Be faithful over what you can do, then God will set you over what you can't...

Be faithful in controlling your thoughts while you are awake... And when God sees your faithfulness, He will set you over the dreams that come against your will and you can't control...

Be faithful over one talent, God will set you over ten or the reward of the one who was set over the ten talents.

Be faithful over combats that come from the outside, then God will set you over springs of spiritual contemplation that flow in your thoughts and heart from the inside.

Be faithful over your loyalty to Leah, God will set you over Rachel. Have sympathy towards the son of Hagar, God will grant you a son for Sarah. Rid yourself of the Sinai wilderness, then God will enable you to enter Canaan.

When you are faithful over the house of Potiphar, God will set you over the palace of Pharoah and all the treasures of Egypt... Be faithful over the palace of Artaxerxes, God will set you over building His temple in Jerusalem... (Nehemiah).

Be faithful to God over the seen things, God will set you over the unseen, over what no ear heard, nor have entered into the heart of man...

God is testing your faithfulness over anything. It could be a simple commandment or one fruit that you abstain from ...

If you proved to be faithful over the Tree of Knowledge, then God will set you over the Tree of Life and the hidden Manna.

Do not belittle the few talents that you possess, but be faithful over them; God is not going to look if you have little or much, but to your faithfulness over them...

According to your faithfulness, God will reward you...

Anba Abraam, Bishop of El-Fayoum, was faithful over merciful deeds and whatever money he had. God set him over an extended range of mercy, including healing the sick and casting out devils.

76.   THE WHOLE TRUTH

The talk about God's love might make you joyful, while the talk about his justice troubles you. However, you have to face the whole truth.

This is the divine truth... that does not separate God's justice from God's love. God's justice is merciful and God's mercy is just. God's justice is full of mercy and His mercy is full of justice...

The two together are the whole truth, the complete truth...

We do not act in spiritual matters according to half the truth...

Articles about hope might cheer you up but you would be troubled by articles about righteousness, purity, the Commandments and the duties required of you.

No matter how you try to avoid the talk about purity, you are required to possess it whether you listened or not. You have to put the whole truth before your eyes. Rejoice in God's commandment like David who found it light for the eyes.

You have to know the whole truth and face it, whatever comforts you or moves you to tears.

No matter how difficult the commandment looks in your eyes, face it. It is God's grace which is in you that will help you to carry it out.

The Lord Jesus also followed the way of the whole truth with us. He told us, "In the world you will have tribulation." This is half the truth. The other half follows, *"But be of good cheer, I have overcome the world."* (John 16:33).

Therefore, we do not escape from the phrase, "You will have tribulation" and be comforted by leaving it out. No, we remember it, no matter how difficult it gets. But we also remember its second half, "Be of good cheer, I have overcome the world."...

In spite of the importance of the work of the Holy Spirit, it is still half the truth. The other half is our part by sharing in the work.

Half the truth is the great salvation granted to us by christ.

The other half is how to obtain the salvation.

Half the truth is that you are God's son. The other half is that he who is born of God does not sin.

This is the whole truth….

✣ ✣ ✣

77. HOW TO CONFESS

Confession is not to sit and tell stories. You might spend a long time talking about your tales with people, without referring to what wrong you have done!

But confession is to judge yourself...

It is condemning yourself in front of God and within the hearing of a priest...

You say: I sinned by doing this and that...

Confession is not to complain about others and to explain people's wrong doings to you. It is to condemn yourself...

Therefore, confession is not to sit with your confession father and blame him and reproach him for neglecting to visit you or direct you, how he did not follow your case or ask about you or give you any spiritual training. In all this you are not judging yourself or referring to your faults... you are in fact judging your confession father!!

Confession is not just being freed of old sins to fall in new ones, without changing your spiritual state.

Confession means repentance, therefore it is called the Sacrament of Repentance.

Confession is not determining in your heart to do something and asking your confession father to agree with you. Otherwise you become upset and persist in asking for his approval, pretending that you are not acting according to your wish, but on the advice of your confession father!!

Confession is to explain your case and humbly ask for guidance. Confession is not just sitting with the priest anywhere, even in a friendly way. It is not a matter of talking to him and letting him use his intelligence to guess what fault you fell in.

Confession is a holy sacrament that has its reverence. In practising it, you feel that you regret what you did and confess to God your sins, while the priest is listening.

Confession is to sit with yourself first, to examine and know all its faults and weaknesses. Then you rebuke yourself for all of that and determine to lead a virtuous life, asking for God's help...

Then, you come to your confession father with a contrite heart. You tell him what you have done wrong, ask for forgiveness and remission, seek advice and guidance and prayer for yourself...

✛ ✛ ✛

78. CONTEMPLATION ON THE EPIPHANY (EL GHETAS)

Adam sinned and did not ask for forgiveness or seek it...

As for the Lord Jesus Christ, the Holy and the only one without sin, **He stood in front of the Baptist as a repentant, representing Adam and his descendants. The Lord offered on their behalf, a baptism of repentance in its most sublime form.**

He carried their sins not only during his crucifixion, but in His life as a Son of Man. Therefore, God was pleased with Him and said, *"This is my beloved Son, in whom I am well pleased."* (Matt. 3:17).

It does not please God to see one justifying himself, finding excuses as Adam and Eve did. Instead of judging themselves in front of God they started blaming someone else.

The Lord Jesus did not blame anyone. He took the sin of another, carried it instead of him and offered a baptism of repentance. Therefore, He pleased the Father who said, *"This is my beloved Son, in whom I am well pleased."* (Matt. 3:17).

The one who is without sin, carried sin for our sake... He did not feel ashamed to walk forward with the sinners and ask his servant, John, to baptise Him. When the great prophet became shy of the situation, He gently said to him, *"Permit it to be so now, for thus it is fitting for us to fulfil all righteousness."* (Matt. 3:15).

By doing this He gave us a practical lesson. **He gave a lesson to carry the sins of others...**

To happily pay the price on their behalf...

Not to justify ourselves, no matter how innocent we are...

And by this we fulfil all righteousness...

Would you be able to train yourself to gain this virtue?

St. John Chrysostom says, "If you are unable to carry the sins of others and relate them to yourself, try at least not to judge another and let him carry your sins...

If we fall to carry the sins of other people, try at least to endure their failings towards us and forgive them...

In this manner, we become like Christ and become worthy of being called sons of God. And with the same kindness that we deal with people, God is going to deal with us...

✛ ✛ ✛

79.   VIOLENCE OR FIRMNESS

Many, in their behaviour, mix violence and firmness.

Firmness is acceptable, when needed but violence is disliked...

When Rehoboam consulted the elders and the young men, the elders advised him to take a gentle and good stand while the young men advised him to be violent.   He followed the suggestion of violence and lost much and the kingdom scattered. (1 Kin. 12:6).   And so failed the policy of violence that Rehoboam followed.

God stood up against the violence of Pharoah.   Owing to this violence, the people's cry was heard by God and He saved them.

Esau and Jacob were brothers.   Esau was a model of violence while Jacob was gentle and quiet.   The Bible says that God loved Jacob, even before his birth...

A violent person might have cruelty in the heart, but the gentle is always distinguished by compassion, love and kindness.

A violent person might have inner pride supporting his violence. As for the gentle, he is usually humble in his ways.

God praised gentleness and humility by saying, *"...and learn from Me, for I am gentle and lowly in heart."* (Matt. 11:29).

Violence could enable you to control people by force and silence them. But it will never make you gain their love.

It is fit to use violence to control the evil who need to be curbed for fear of them harming others. But it is not fit to use it in dealing with those who are quiet and gentle. Violence also fails completely with those who are sensitive.

Violence is the last resort of the wise, when all other quiet means fail.

There is a big difference between "a violent person" with whom violence becomes part of his nature and another person who is generally quiet but turns to violence for necessity, when nothing else works. This is called firmness...

Sometimes, there is firmness with violence...

80.   TWO LEVELS

In the life of virtue, there are levels. Here we refer to two:

The spiritual level and the social level.

A person who is spiritually distinguished must be socially distinguished. A social person, however, does not necessarily have to be spiritual.

A social person might be able to gain the love of those around him, by means the spiritual person cannot handle. It could be through jokes or entertainment... or a way of flattery or lying. He might help others by using means that the conscience of a spiritual person would not accept...

Therefore, a social person succeeds in gaining people by non-spiritual means...

A spiritual person likes gaining people but in a way that does not make him lose God or lose his purity...

Therefore, there are differences in measuring what is fit or unfit...

The aim of a spiritual person is not just to gain people for himself, but for God before anything. The spirituality means much to him, just as his own spirituality.

An idealistic person combines both levels together:

He is socially successful, loved by all, at the same time, he uses a correct spiritual and faultless way.

It is easy for a spiritual person to train himself to be silent so that he would not err by the tongue... Stronger than him is the spiritual person who talks, not only without fault, but in a positive way to benefit others. He is a tactful speaker whose talk people enjoy...

It is quite easy for a spiritual person to abstain from joking and become always serious. Few will be able to harmonise with his continual seriousness. They will be pleased to see a spiritual person who is at the same time cheerful and happy, laughs with them without any fault on his side or theirs.

Spirituality does not mean being grave, it turns people off...

Spirituality has nothing to do with isolation from society and its faults. Otherwise, religion would not be good for society...

To become adapted to society is a side of spirituality. It is a higher level than the social. It is not wise for some to put it on a lower level, or else that could be one way of self-centeredness...

✠ ✠ ✠

81.   LITTLE AND MUCH

One of the well known sayings is: "The little that is permanent is better than the much which is irregular.

This is also good for the spiritual life.

Many take very quick, high leaps starting with what is more than their capabilities. They fail to carry on, so they regress. The result is falling into depression and despair...

The correct spiritual position is for one to start with whatever is within his capability, because the little that is permanent gives stability to the spiritual life.

Many are those who do not remain firm due to confusion. It proves lack of organisation and failure in following a wise advice.

Whoever fasts in a moderate way grows little by little, till he reaches a strong spiritual level... This is better than starting with a high level that he would not be able cope with, then gradually slide down as if he never started at all.

We mean by "the little" what is within your capacity, not the little that is due to idleness.

God is able to bless the little and make it grow...

In you spirituality, you must walk on solid grounds. You take the step that there is return from. But you pass it to another and with every step, you gain experience ...

82.   THE BENEFIT

Many ask for a word of benefit. But do they all benefit from it?

Benefit has undoubtedly two sources:

Firstly: that the word is beneficial, good for construction.

Secondly: that the listener is the type of person who benefits.

The one who loves to benefit could benefit even from a word of rebuke, a hard word or even a word that is said to another person, not to him...

We still benefit from words that our Fathers said to people who lived at their time, not ours...

The words of benefit are available: if we honestly want them, we will find them within our, reach... The books are full of words of benefit and the mouths of guides flow with life, for those who want life...

Therefore, after the Lord Jesus said words of benefit to all the Angels of the seven churches, He immediately said, *"He who has ears to hear, let him hear!"* (Rev. 2,3).

A word of benefit needs an ear to hear, needs the love of benefit and an effective will to cooperate with such love...

Knowing words of benefit is not enough. In fact, knowledge on its own is judgement, because, "He who knows more has more expected from him"... and the Lord said, "... the word that I have spoken will judge them in the last day."

Some heard the Lord Jesus and did not benefit from what they heard. One of them even went away sorrowful...

Many heard and liked the word, but did not put it into action.

Others heard St. Paul, the Apostle and said, "what does this babbler want to say?!" And they did not benefit, even from St. Paul's talk.

The word of benefit was there, but without benefit!

Our mother Eve heard the word from God and repeated it literally, but did not benefit. In fact, she fell on the same day...

People ask for a word of benefit. But is the benefit gained just by talk?! ...

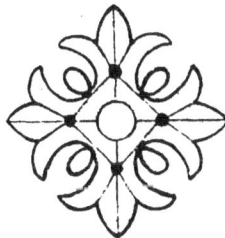

83.   FORMALITIES

Many people, in their worship and relationship with God, pay more attention to the formalities and forget the essence.

In prayer, for example, they stand in front of God and talk to Him, paying more attention to the words and their length. This is a formality as the essence of prayer is the relationship that links Man to God. It is the feeling that one is in the presence of the Divinity...

In fasting, some concentrate on the period of abstaining from eating and the type of food they eat. This is also a formality. The essence of fasting is mainly the principle of prevention and overruling oneself, controlling the body and rising above the level of materialism and food. That is what escapes many.

In preparation to receive the Holy Communion, many are more concerned with the cleanliness of the body in a very formal way, with no attention to the essence of purity, physically and spiritually!...

In reading the Holy Bible, the main concern of some is the amount they read and the regularity to do so.   This is formality... but the essence is reading with understanding and contemplation. It is a matter of going beyond the meaning and turning the action of reading into spirit and life...

Some people enter the monastic life and give more care to the outside appearance such as prostration and its number, fasting and abstaining from eating for long periods, locking oneself in the cell, remaining silent and neglecting one's clothes... As for purity of the heart deep from inside real death to the world and the object of monasticism in being occupied with God and His love, it is forgotten amidst the concern with formalities!...

The service is very often lost because of the formalities. We might become completely involved in what we are going to say... The effect of what we say in changing people's hearts and leading them to the love of God, is forgotten by many... The service might have several activities, organisations and prominent names. These are all types of formalities. The depth in the service is known, it is the aim of serving, that is the salvation of souls... But where is it?!

Formalities never build the Kingdom. It reminds us of what the Lord said about the Pharisees and Scribes, "...who cleanse the outside of the cup and the dish..." They have been compared to tombs that are white from the outside and the inside is exactly the opposite...

God does not take notice of formalities, therefore He said, *"My son, give me your heart."* (Prov. 23:26). For this reason the commandment is not taken literally but God is mainly concerned about the love that is in it. As for love, God said, *"On love hangs all the Law and the Prophets."* (Matt. 22:40).

84. TEMPTATIONS

Many temptations happen because of the envy of the devil...

If the devil finds a highly spiritual person, he becomes furious and envious. He attacks him with temptations to see how firm he is in the life of the spirit...

That is what happened with the Lord Jesus Christ...

The devil was not happy about the great glory that the Lord Jesus received at the Jordan River, where the Father witnessed for Him saying, *"This is my beloved Son, in who I am well pleased."* (Matt. 3:17). Then the Holy Spirit descended on Him as a dove. Also, John the Baptist witnessed for Jesus saying, *"...whose sandal-strap I am not worthy to stoop down and unloose."* (Mark 1:7) ... Therefore, the devil followed the Lord with temptations on the mountain.

The devil's combat sometimes proves the success of the spiritual work, which makes one confident in his work.

The devil's temptations are divided into two types: Tribulations and enticement...

Tribulations do not hurt, but one can benefit from them and learn patience. They enable us to experience God's help. St. James, the Apostle said, *"My brethren, count it all joy when you fall into various trials."* (James 1:2).

But the trouble is in the trial by sin...

A sin could tempt the faithful to do or think in a harsh way. In spite of his refusal, it continues fighting him till he cries to God saying, "lead us not into temptation......"

Temptations indicate that the devil does not give up...

He does not give up, no matter how long it takes. He kept on tempting the Lord Jesus for forty days. And in spite of his failure and God dismissing him, he left for a while then returned to tempt Him, even when the Lord was on the cross.

We do not fear the devils' combats.

The grace within us is much stronger than all the tricks of the devil. And the Holy Spirit that works within us is able to defeat the devil. Besides, God gave us authority over all the devils...

As the Lord Jesus Christ has triumphed over all trials of the devil, He gave our human nature the spirit of victory and became our leader in His procession of triumph.

May the Lord be blessed in our trials as in our worship...

✠ ✠ ✠

85. EVERYTHING FOR YOUR SPIRITUALITY

God created everything for your spirituality...

Heaven and earth are not for your materialistic benefit. They are also for your spiritual benefit, if you are able to extract the spiritual lessons they offer you. *"The heavens declare the glory of God and the firmament shows his handiwork."* (Ps. 19:1).

The Bible is not only for religious knowledge. It is also for your spiritual growth.......*"The words that I speak to you are spirit and they are life."* (John 6:63). There is a big difference in reading the Bible for study and reading it for a spiritual benefit.

Service, also, is not just education. Education is merely a means to lead to the spiritualities. Therefore there is a difference between one type of education and another.

There is an education that addresses your' mind and another education that fills your heart. One education turns you into a learned man and the other turns you into a worshipper...

The education that you undertake is not only for the spirituality of others but also for your own spirituality.

You benefit as much as your listeners benefit. If you do not benefit with them, they surely would not benefit from what you said since the talk would have lost its spiritual effect.

Hymns and chants at church are not just music and tunes. They are prayers directed to God. They have their depth and effect on your heart and your spirituality...

Therefore, there is a difference between the one who just sings and the one who chants hymns.

The same applies to all the spiritual means...

Even all the incidents you experience are permitted by God so you can gain a spiritual benefit from them...

There are those who become nervously, psychologically or mentally affected by incidents. Others are affected spiritually by whatever events they experience; everything that happens to them makes them closer to God....

The people that you meet, are sent by God. Passing your way, they are for your own spiritual benefit, if you know how to benefit from them.

The righteous present you with an example and a blessing, while you benefit endurance, patience and forgiveness for others from evil.

✣ ✣ ✣

86. REPENTANCE AND ITS PERFECTION

Repentance has levels and steps that one follows:

1. The first step is the feeling of being in a bad condition and the desire to change it. It is like what happened to the prodigal son, who came to himself and found that he is about to die of starvation. He found that the perfect solution is to return to his Father.

2. The second step is leaving sin and keeping away from all the ways that lead to it. What is meant by leaving sin is not to leave a particular sin but sin in general. At this point one starts to discover himself.

The more one grows in the spirit, the more he discovers new faults that he never realised before. Then he tries to eradicate them. He needs to pass various stages of purifying the self, till it returns to God's image.

3. In a life of repentance, leaving sin must be permanent and firm, with no return, so was the repentance of the Saints. We never heard that Augustine returned to sin once more. The same with Moses the Black, Mary the Egyptian and Pelagia.

Repentance, in the lives of all these Saints was a confirmed turn to God without returning to sin.

4. The perfection of repentance, as the Saints said, is not just leaving sin, but hating it.

The one who actually leaves sin, but continues longing for it in his heart, has not really repented. His heart has not yet repented. He is bound to have a relapse with action as well. Nevertheless, the heart is the basis. And the Lord says, *"My Son, give me your heart."* (Prov. 23:26). Thus repentance must be from the heart and the heart becomes entirely for God.

5.   Such a repentant person cannot sin again, because all his feelings and desires become opposed to sin and would not accept it. Besides, he would not need to strive to keep away from sin. He automatically stays away from it because of his hatred to it.

6.   Real repentance must have fruits.

As the Bible says, *"Therefore bear fruits worthy of repentance."* (Matt. 3:8). The first of these fruits is love for God which possesses the heart, changes the life and bears fruits of righteousness.

87.   GOD'S LOVE FOR US "A"

How great is God's love for us. It's enough to say that God is Love... And *"we love Him because He first loved us."* (1 John 4:19).

He loved us before we were, therefore He created us...

Because of His love for us, He created us after His image and likeness.

He prepared everything for us before we were created. He raised the Heaven to be a roof and paved the Earth so we can walk on it. He made the light, water, plants and paradise... Then He created us.

When we fell in sin, He prepared for us a way of salvation.

Due to His love for us, He sent prophets to guide us and gave us a conscience and a written Law to enlighten our insights.

It was His love for us that made Him incarnate, take our nature and bless this nature in Him. On our behalf, He obeyed the Law and pleased God the Father by presenting a God-fearing image of humanity.

Due to His love, He died for us, *"The just for the unjust."* (1 Pet. 3:18).

He became a love-offering on the Cross. He carried the sin of the whole world and washed it with His blood. "The One without sin was considered sinful, for our sake," and paid the whole price one our behalf.

"... Having loved His own who were in the world, He loved them to the end." (John 13:1). And, *"Greater love has no one than this, to lay down his life for his friends."* (John 15:13).

Because He loved us, He said, *"No longer do I call you servants, but I have called you friends."* (John 15:15). He also called us brethren and, *"... in all things He had to be made like His brethren."* (Heb. 2:17). We became sons of the Heavenly Father, *"Behold what manner of love the Father has bestowed on us, that we should be called children of God."* (1 John 3:1).

To show His love for us, He said, *"... I am with you always, even to the end of the age."* (Matt. 28:20). *"For where two or three are gathered together in my name, I am there in the midst of them."* (Matt. 18:20).

His love is also shown in His protection, care and guidance for us in everything.

88. GOD'S LOVE FOR US "B"

Owing to God's love for us, He considers us part of Him, as He says, *"I am the vine, you are the branches."* (John 15:5). He also says, *"...we are members of His body."* (Eph. 5:30), or He is the head and the whole Church is the body. Again He says, *"Abide in me and I in you, as the branches abide, in the vine."* (John 15:4). He also says about us to the Father, *"I in them and you in me, that they may be made perfect in one."* (John 17:23).

✧ How beautiful is the expression in the Bible about God's love for us, in saying, *"... partakers of the divine nature."* (2 Pet. 1:4). And also, *"... the communion of the Holy Spirit."* (2 Cor. 13:14). Of course it is not a communion in the nature and essence but in work. Therefore, St. Paul says about himself and his friend Silas, *"For we are God's fellow workers. " "For we are God's fellow workers."* (1 Cor. 3:9).

✧ **One of the aspects of God's love for us is the friendship that developed between Him and our human race.** For example, Abraham was called, "El-Khalil" the friend of God and Enoch, about whom it was said, *"And Enoch walked with God; and he was not for God took him."* (Gen. 5:24). Moses, too spent forty days with God on the mountain. The twelve Disciples are also another example, the way the Lord associated with them...

✛ **It is also beautiful how God made His delight in the sons of men...**

He, the unlimited, humbled Himself for the human beings, who are limited and associated with them. He also appeared to them and talked to them mouth to ear.

✛ **It is also due to God's love for us all that these amazing ways of care** which history tells us occurred, such as the split of the Red Sea, the Manna in the wilderness, the water flowing from a rock, looking after Elijah during the famine, delivering Peter from prison and Daniel from the lions' den and the three youths from the burning furnace...beside many other stories that have no end.

✛ **As a sign of God's love for us** He has given us these beautiful promises:

"I have, inscribed you on the palms of my hands." (Is. 49:16), *"But the very hairs of your head are all numbered."* (Matt. 10:30), *"I will give you a new heart,"* (Ezek. 36:26). *"And no one is able to snatch them out of My Father's hand."* (John 10:29) and, *"I go to prepare a place for you."* (John 14:2).

✛ **The gifts we are granted are an evidence of God's love for Man.**

The gift of eternity, of the resurrection as in the body of His glory and the several gifts of the Holy Spirit... Blessed by God in His love.

✛✛✛

89.   LOVE SACRIFICES

Love is tested through suffering, tribulation and sacrifice.

The one who is not able to sacrifice is the one who does not love... Once he loves, he will sacrifice everything.

Abraham, the father of fathers, because of his love for God, left his people and the house of his father and lived a stranger in a tent...

But Abraham's love for God reached its peak when he laid his only son on the altar. He placed wood and fire around him and raised his hand with the knife, to sacrifice him.

When Daniel loved the Lord, he sacrificed himself and accepted being thrown into the lions' den. The same with the three youths who proved their love through self sacrifice, to be cast into the burning furnace...

St. Paul, the Apostle, said about his love for the Lord Jesus, *"I have suffered the loss of all things and count them as rubbish, that I may gain Christ and be found in Him."* (Phil. 3:8-9).

Our fathers the martyrs and the confessors, because of their love for God, sacrificed their blood, their lives and comfort. They experienced torment and never feared, because of their great love...

There are obstacles that hinder Man from sacrifice: his love of comfort, love of dignity and the love of self... But real love does not care for comfort, pride or self...

One sacrifices everything for the sake of the one he loves...

Jacob, the father of fathers, when he fell in love with Rachel, sacrificed much for her sake. He toiled for twenty years, with the sun burning him during the day and the cold at night... He considered all these years as a few days because of his love for her.

What have you sacrificed for Jesus, who sacrificed Himself on the Cross for your sake?...

The one who loves, sacrifices himself for God and for people.

He has to practise first to sacrifice what is outside himself, such as wealth, time and possessions. But the one who is unable to sacrifice what is outside himself, how would he sacrifice himself?!

If you are unable to sacrifice, then you do not love others; or do you only love yourself...

✠ ✠ ✠

90.   GOD'S SOLUTIONS

Truly God has many solutions...

We think of our problems, using our human mind, which is limited. As for God He is unlimited in His knowledge and His wisdom.

When matters become complicated, their complication is relative for us human beings. As for God nothing becomes complicated, everything is easy and the solutions are many.

God interferes at the right time and in the suitable way. It could be a solution that never crossed our minds, one that we never thought of or expected...

"The things which are impossible, with man are possible with God." (Luke 18:27).

With God, everything is possible, nothing is hard, as Job the righteous said, *"And that no purpose of yours can be withheld from you."* (Job 42:2).

God controls everything, sees everything and nothing is hidden from Him. He plans in secret or in the dark. Everything is uncovered before His eyes and the answer is known.

Therefore, it is good what Moses the Prophet said, *"Stand still and see the salvation of the Lord. The Lord will fight for you and you shall hold your peace."* (Ex. 14:13-14).

God's solutions are strong and His salvation is great...

The faithful wait hoping for God's salvation and they rejoice in hope...

God's work for them in past days increases their faith in God's doings now, in the future and at all time...

God is God. He does not change in His love or His care...

Therefore, it is said in the psalm, *"The Lord shall preserve you from all evil, He shall preserve your soul. The Lord shall preserve your going out and your coming in."* (Ps. 121:7-8).

In our life we deal with God, not with people. We are all in His hands. Nobody is independent of God or outside His dominion.

Therefore we are confident in God's work with us...

We are sure of His interference, listening to the psalmist saying, "Wait for the Lord. Be strong and comfort your heart. Wait for the Lord."

May God's name be blessed forever.

✠ ✠ ✠

91.   GOD EXISTS

A problem, by itself, without God, could cause trouble for some. But the problem, with the presence of God, would not cause trouble...

Hope in God and His interference gives the heart joy and confidence. As the Apostle said, *"Rejoicing in hope."* (Rom. 12:12).

✢   **Was the lions' den fearful to Daniel?** Surely it was not, as far as he knew the phrase, *"My God sent his Angel and shut the lions' mouths."* (Dan. 6:22).

✢   **Was the fiery furnace a source of loss for the three youths?** No it was a different case, with a "fourth" like the Son of God, walking with them in the midst of the fire.

✢   **Did Goliath, the giant, look fearful to David?** He was like that to the army of soldiers who faced Goliath without God. As for David, he was strong and did not fear Goliath and his threats because he had God with him in the battle. He said, *"For the battle is the Lord's. But I come to you in the name of the Lord of Hosts. This day the Lord will deliver you into my hand."* (1 Sam. 17:48).

Our feeling that God is with us is the reason of our confidence. God's name is a strong fortress that the righteous take for a refuge.

"The Lord shall preserve you from all evil, He shall preserve your soul. *The Lord shall preserve your going out and your coming in."* (Ps. 121:7-8).

"I have set the Lord always before me; because He is my right hand and I shall not be moved." (Ps. 16:8).

Truly, letting God in a problem solves it...

✧ **In God's name, Elijah faced Ahab.**

And in God's name, Moses and Aaron faced Pharaoh... And in God's name, Paul faced Festus and Agrippa.

✧ The Lord was the strength for these Saints and others like them.

The Psalmist said, *"The Lord is my strength and song and He has become my salvation."* (Ps. 118:18). And, *"The Lord is my light and my salvation."* (Ps. 27:1).

✧ We deal with God and not with people... We set God in front of us in all our problems and He gives us strength.

If you weaken one day, it means you forgot God's strength.

✧ ✧ ✧

92.   ANOTHER VIEW

We look at matters in a specific way and from a special angle and see them from a certain point of view. But what we see is not everything.

There is another view through faith, that agrees with what God sees.

✢   What do we see in Joseph being sold as a slave by his brothers?

What do we see in his imprisonment after all his loyalty while in Potiphar's house?

All we can see is evil, jealousy and betrayal...

We also see injustice and ill-fate.

As for God, He has another view of all these matters.

That was the way for Joseph to be glorified.

How would we describe what Judas Iscariot did except betrayal in the lowest form?!

The way Pontius Pilate acted, could it be anything but cowardice, injustice and yielding to evil?!

What would we say about Annas and Caiaphas except envy, lying and conspiracy?!

We look at these things and say they should not have happened.

But God has another view.

He could see the Salvation as a result of the Crucifixion which was caused by all of these people.

It is God, who changes evil into goodness.

It does not mean that their evil was good!

Of course not, but the other view is that God is able to make sweet out of the bitter and make all matters happen for the glory of His Holy name.

✛   Jonah boarded the ship but a mighty tempest was about to turn it over. The mariners threw the cargo into the sea and were afraid... Was that all evil? Or was there another view of this sea tragedy?

The other view was that the waves of the raging sea caused the mariners to believe in the Lord.

✛   **There is no doubt that we have limited sight... You might he able to see the tribulation but not the blessing that God will positively achieve as a result of this trial.**

But through faith we see the blessing, trusting that, *".. all things work together for good to those who love God."* (Rom. 8:28).

✛✛✛

93.   SINCERITY

Sincerity is purity of love, truth of emotion and feelings of loyalty presented by someone you trust in his friendship.

Sincerity shows during tribulations and its metal is tested at a time of distress.

In such sincerity St. Peter said to the Lord Jesus, *"If I have to die with you, I will not deny you!"* (Mark 14:31). And the Lord Jesus said to His Disciples, *"But you are those who have continued with me in my trial."* (Luke 22:28).

With this sincerity, the Marys and John, the beloved, stood around Jesus during the crucifixion. And with the same sincerity Joseph of Arimathea asked Pilate that he might take the body of Jesus to be shrouded with the help of Nicodemus.

Through their sincerity, none of these people gave a thought to what might be said about them or what might happen.

Sincerity is characterised by sacrifice. One might forget himself and remember nothing, except his love and the one who he loves.

The Bible tells us about Ruth's sincerity towards her mother-in-law, Naomi and how she said to her, *"wherever you go, I will go, where you die, I will die."* (Ruth 1:16).

Jonathan lived with David in sincerity, even enduring his father's reproach and anger, because of his love for David.

And with the same sincerity, David was good to all the members of Jonathan's family after his death.

With sincerity, the martyrs offered themselves for the love of Christ. The Confessors endured all types of torment for the Lord's sake...

There are those who were sincere to their families, their teachers, their spiritual and worldly fathers, their nations or to specific principles they lived with... It was sincerity till death.

There are other types of sincerity, such as the doctor to his patient, the lawyer to his client, the teacher to his students, the writer to his readers and the guard to those whom he is protecting.

Some are sincere because of their duty and conscience, others because of love and loyalty and some because sincerity is part of their nature. They treat everyone with the same sincerity, especially those they love.

How beautiful is sincerity. It is nobility, love and a golden crown...

✠ ✠ ✠

94.   THE PEACE OF THE CHURCH

The most repeated prayer in our liturgy is litany for the Church's peace, in which we say, "Remember, O Lord, the peace of Your One, Holy, Universal and Apostolic Church. Preserve her in peace."

We pray it at the beginning of all the Litanies and in the raising of incense during Vespers, the early morning raising of incense and in every circuit the Priest performs around the Altar while praying the Litanies.

At the beginning of Mass, during the Offertory, we pray saying, "Grant peace and holiness to the One, Holy, Universal and Apostolic Church of God." We also pray the same litany during the ordination of Priests.

In the litany of the King or President, we also pray for the peace of the Church saying, "Touch his heart, for the peace of Your One, Holy, Universal and Apostolic Church."

The peace of the Church was one of the most important concerns of our Fathers the Apostles and all the Saints.

For all of them, the Church represented the Kingdom of God on earth, which will be extended to the Heavenly Kingdom.

It represents the source of faith and God's dwelling with the people.

Its peace and safety are the essence of everybody's prayer, more than one prays for his own requests. It is the centre of contemplation in the Lord's prayer, in which we say, "Hallowed by your name. Your Kingdom come. Your will be done.."

Praying for the peace of the Church is the prayer that survived for centuries, in the mouth of the Faithful, shepherds and flock, clergy and congregation. Even in the liturgy for the ordination of monks who split themselves from the world, we pray for the peace of the Church.

It was beautiful of St. Paul the first hermit, the greatest of the solitaries and spirit-borne, to ask St. Anthony about the peace of the Church.

It is a prayer that we pray from the depths of our hearts.

Not just as part of the liturgy, but as living and burning feelings.

Let everyone expend all his emotions in this prayer. Amen.

✤✤✤

95.   CAUSING OTHERS TO STUMBLE

A stumble is a fall. The one who causes others to stumble is the one who causes the fall of others, either by action or by thought.

The Lord Jesus Christ said, *"It is impossible that no offences should come but woe to him through whom they come! It would be better for him if a millstone were hung around his neck and he were thrown into the sea, than that he should offend one of these little ones."* (Luke 17:1-2).

The little ones could be young either in age or in thought and the ability to distinguish. They could also be little in soul or in faith or in their spiritual level, so that any offending action may trouble them.

Very often, older members of the family talk in the presence of children, with words not suitable for children to hear. They think that the children do not understand, but most probably it offends them or remains in their minds.

The same thing happens when parents fight or argue in front of their little children. It offends them since they expect adults to be idealistic. Divorce also causes offence to children.

There are several means of entertainment that a family buys, then they tempt the children to sin: It could be a radio or television programme or some magazines or books. Certain parties held by the family could also be offensive for their children.

The bad example also tempts the little ones to sin either in words, deeds, clothes or the type of treatment.

Often children learn lying from members of their own family. They also learn to make fun of others and to exaggerate. They might even imitate their actions, expressions and voices. Children are fond of imitating.

The temptation to sin or fall might come from education and thoughts that the children receive from adults. It could happen at home, at school or from neighbours. It is the type of education that implants subversive ideas or creates wrong feelings of hatred towards some people.

If the principles taught to a child by different people, contradict each other, the child will suffer from confusion, conflict and doubt. This contradiction or clash of views in education would cause the child to stumble.

The little ones are put in our trust. If we fail to implant good in them at least avoid offending them...

✛✛✛

96.   THE GLORY OF SUFFERING

St. Paul, the Apostle, says in his Epistle to the Romans, *"If indeed we suffer with Him, that we may also be glorified together."* (Rom. 8:17).

Thus, suffering for the Lord becomes a measure of the glory that awaits the faithful in the eternal Kingdom.

Therefore, the Church places the martyrs above all the Saints.

They are mentioned in the Church's prayers before the spirit-borne and the solitary fathers, who filled the wilderness with prayers and contemplation. They are also mentioned before our fathers the Patriarchs and Bishops, with all their services in spreading the Word. This is all because of the sufferings they endured for the sake of God.

Even in service, the measure of suffering is also obvious, as the Apostle says, *"... and each will receive his own reward according to his own labour."* (1 Cor. 3:8). Therefore, the Lord says in his letter to the Angel of the Church at Ephesus, *"I know your works, your labour, your patience... and you have persevered and have patience and have laboured for my name's sake and have not become weary."* (Rev. 2:2-3), putting labour at the beginning.

It is also said in the Bible that, *"God is not unjust to forget your work and labour of love..."*(Heb. 6:10).

Love expresses its existence by labouring for the beloved one, as the Apostle says, *"... Let us not love in word or in tongue."* (1 John 3:18).

The depth of love also shows in suffering, when the level of love is raised up to sacrifice and redemption.

Therefore, God's love was shown to us in its deepest form when the Lord was on the Cross, sacrificing himself for our redemption, the just for the unjust.

Christ was at the peak of His glory when He was in His deepest passion.

For this reason, He said about his crucifixion, *"Now the Son of Man is glorified."* (John 13:13). The picture of His crucifixion is the picture of His glory...

St. Paul, the Apostle, considers suffering as a gift from God. In this, he says, *"For to you it has been granted on behalf of Christ, not only to believe in Him, but also to suffer for his sake."* (Phil. 1:29).

St. Peter, the Apostle, also talked about suffering saying, *"For to this you were called, because Christ also suffered for us, leaving us an example, that you should follow his steps."* (1 Pet. 2:21).

✙ ✙ ✙

97. THE ASCENSION

The Lord ascended in glory, defying all the law of gravity. **He also gave us hope of being lifted up like Him, defying the law of gravity and joining Him,** by saying, *"And I, if I am lifted up from the earth, will draw all people to myself."* (John 12:32).

He was lifted up on a cloud and disappeared from their sight. But He will come again on the clouds of Heaven, with His Angels and Saints, to lift us up on the clouds with Him and be with God all the time.

As He sat down at the right hand of the Father, we will sit down with Him in His glory.

The One they crucified at Golgotha and was counted as a sinner, enduring many reproaches and insults, has risen from the dead in glory, ascended to Heaven in glory and sat down at the right hand of the Father in glory.

Golgotha was not a sad ending of His life. It was the beginning of His glory.

Therefore, whoever suffers with Him will surely be glorified with Him...

The Ascension was the last picture of the Lord seen by His Disciples. It lifted up their eyes to where Christ is sitting down. It is what the Apostle meant when he said, *"Received up in glory."* (1 Tim. 3:16).

Thus Christian suffering became inseparable from its glory.

Christ who suffered for our sake, appeared to St. Stephen during the suffering of his martyrdom "He gazed into heaven and saw the glory of God and Jesus standing at the right hand of God and said, Look, I see the heavens opened and the Son of Man standing at the right hand of God. He then cried out with a loud voice, "Lord Jesus, receive my spirit."

The one who descended has also ascended...

We too, would not be able to ascend, if we do not first descend...

We, also, must humble ourselves, endure suffering and he lifted up on the cross, before the ascension to the right hand of the Father...

As Christ has been lifted up, we always lift up our eyes to where Christ sits on the right hand of the Father, till he comes back once more on the clouds, to take us to Him.

Then, we will he lifted up with no descent... Amen.

✛ ✛ ✛

98. THE APOSTLES FAST

Nobody should think lightly of the Fast of the Apostles', as it is the most ancient fast the Christian Church has known through generations. The Lord referred to it by saying, *"But the days will come when the bridegroom will be taken away from them and they will fast."* (Matt. 9:15).

Our Fathers, the Apostles, started their service by fasting. The Lord Himself started His service by fasting forty days on the mountain.

The Apostles' Fast, therefore, is dedicated for the service and the Church.

It is said about our teacher, St. Peter, the Apostle, that he fasted, *"...then became very hungry and wanted to eat."* (Acts 10:10). During his hunger, he saw heaven open and saw a vision about the acceptance of the Gentiles.

As their fasting was accompanied by vision and divine guidance, it was also associated with the work and coming of the Holy Spirit. The Bible says, "As they ministered to the Lord and fasted, the Holy Spirit said *"Now separate for me Barnabas and Saul for the work to which I have called them.*

Then, having fasted and prayed and laid hands on them, they sent them away. So being sent out by the Holy Spirit, they went down Seleucia... " (Acts 13:2-4).

There are certain aspects that mark out the fast of our Fathers, the Apostles, such as: fasting, praying, serving and the work of the Holy Spirit.

It pleases us that the Holy Spirit works during fasting...

The divine call also comes during fasting...

Ordination of ministers is done during fasting and ministers start by fasting before they begin their service.

There are fastings related to repentance, such as Jonah's fast and the fast related to humility as mentioned in the book of Joel.

Other fastings are for specific requests, such as Esther's fasting.

Fasting for casting out evil spirits, as the Lord said, *"However this kind does not go out except by prayer and fasting."* (Matt. 17:2 1).

There are fastings before we receive any of the Lord's Graces, in the sacraments such as Baptism, Confirmation (Myron), Holy Communion and Priesthood.

As for the Apostles' Fast, it is for service and the Church, at least to teach us the necessity and benefit of fasting for the service.

We fast that God may interfere in the service and support it. We also fast to serve while we are in a good spiritual condition being aware of our weakness...

How we longed for this fast to come while we were during the Holy Pentecost Season "Khamasein".

99.   A WORD OF BENEFIT

Many search for benefit from a word...

If they do not read it or hear it they feel that they have not benefited!!

✣   The wise person sees a word of benefit in everything.

✣   Even in the silence of others, he sees benefit and wisdom... He might benefit from their silence more than he benefits from their talk.

✣   Every incident you experience in life, your life or the life of others, holds a word of benefit for you... Therefore, many benefit from incidents more than they benefit from books, articles or talks...

✣   Life experience is also full of countless words of benefit, for the one who knows how to benefit from such experience.

For this reason we have been called to benefit from the wisdom of elders as they have experienced much and each experience bears a word of benefit.

✣   Sickness in many cases is a word of benefit in itself...

It whispers in the ear of the sick sayings that are not found in books.

Also, sickness could be a word of benefit for those around the sick person, either relatives, friends or visitors...

✢   Death is also a word of benefit for many well known Saints, such as St. Anthony and St. Paul... many used to visit the tombs to listen to the word of benefit death whispers in people's hearts... while he is silent.

✢   Tribulation is also a word of benefit for those who are good at profiting from it, either the one who experiences it or who witnesses it in others. Do not take from tribulation its trouble but its lessons.

✢   Nature also has words of benefit though it seems to be silent. Therefore we have been asked, in the Bible, to learn from the lilies of the field and birds of the air. Even the lazy can learn form the ant.

✢   The word of benefit is there, nobody is deprived of it. But people generally need the gift of contemplation and depth to be able to extract a word of benefit from whatever comes their way...

It could be either a spoken or a silent word of benefit, written or inferred... he who has ears to hear let him hear...

✢ ✢ ✢

100.   THE LOVE OF ONESELF

The true love of oneself comes by training ourselves to love God, His permanent dwelling in us and our submission to the work of His Spirit...

There is no way for the self to enjoy God's dwelling in it except through purity and humility so it would not resist the work of the Spirit or prefer its own ignorance to the wisdom of God.

In that way, self-love truly shows, in self-denial.

Self-denial in working, where you say, *"'... yet not I, but the grace of God which was with me."* (1 Cor. 15:10).   Self-denial means also abandoning self-praise and honour, *"Not unto us, O Lord, not unto us.   But to your name give Glory."* (Ps. 115:1). Self-denial in striving, where the faithful person sacrifices his comfort and all his wealth to build the Kingdom of God...

Self-denial also shows in dealing with God and with people.

Here, one prefers others to himself in everything, *"in honour giving preference to one another."* (Rom. 12:10).

This is the basis of practical love to all others, not only in honour but also in giving, sacrificing and labouring for the sake of others.   One sacrifices for others' sake to the extent of sacrificing oneself. One would not even object to carrying others' sins and relating them to himself, depriving himself from everything to give others..

Some, however love themselves in a wrong worldly way. While trying to build, they will destroy it and instead of lifting it up, they will lose it.

The Lord Jesus Christ said, *"He who finds his life will lose it and he who loses his life for my sake will find it."* (Matt. 10:39).

Those who left worldly pleasures for the sake of God are considered lost by people of the world, although they have actually found the real way to build the self. Among such people are the monks, the spirit-borne and all those who consecrated themselves to serve the Lord. They are all those who said with Peter, *"...we have left all and followed You."* (Matt. 19:27).

The one who loves himself walks in the narrow path for the sake of God, carrying the Cross every day...

This person does actually love himself...

As for the one who satisfies all his worldly and physical desires, he does not love himself but loves the world and its desires...

✠ ✠ ✠